PACKAGING

IN THE SAME SERIES

Food Cycle Technology Source Books

PACKAGING

Practical Action Publishing Ltd
27a Albert Street, Rugby, CV21 2SG, Warwickshire, UK
www.practicalactionpublishing.org

© The United Nations Development Fund for Women (UNIFEM) 1993, 1996
This edition published in 1996
Transferred to digital printing in 2008

ISBN 978 1 85339 334 1
ISBN Library Ebook: 9781780444222

A catalogue record for this book is available from the British Library.

The contributors have asserted their rights under the Copyright Designs and Patents Act 1988 to be identified as authors of their respective contributions.

Since 1974, Practical Action Publishing has published and disseminated books and information in support of international development work throughout the world. Practical Action Publishing is a trading name of Practical Action Publishing Ltd (Company Reg. No. 1159018), the wholly owned publishing company of Practical Action. Practical Action Publishing trades only in support of its parent charity objectives and any profits are covenanted back to Practical Action (Charity Reg. No. 247257, Group VAT Registration No. 880 9924 76).

Typeset by Dorwyn Ltd, Rowlands Castle, Hants, UK

Contents

Acknowledgements

This series of food cycle technology source books has been prepared for Intermediate Technology (IT) in the United Kingdom within the context of UNIFEM's Women and Food Cycle Technologies specialization.

During the preparation process the project staff have contacted numerous project directors, rural development agencies, technology centres, women's organizations, equipment manufacturers and researchers in all parts of the world.

UNIFEM and IT wish to thank the many agencies and individuals who have contributed to the preparation of this source book. Special thanks are owed to Peggy Oti-Boateng of the Technology Consultancy Centre, University of Science and Technology, Ghana and Barrie Axtell of IT Consultants, UK, who researched and wrote this source book, Clare Sheffield for preparation of the manuscript and Matthew Whitton for the illustrations. In addition to those listed in the Contacts Section, the authors wish to thank: John New of the Natural Resources Institute, UK; Emma Crewe of IT, UK; Kithsiri Dharmapriya of IT, Sri Lanka; Simon Burne of the Panos Institute; Bertha Msora of Ranche House College, Zimbabwe; Abdullah Al-Mahmud of the Mennonite Central Committee, Bangladesh, and Jim McDowell for their invaluable contributions.

The preparation of the source books has been funded by UNIFEM with a cost-sharing contribution from the governments of the Netherlands and Italy. UNIFEM is also grateful to the government of Italy for providing the funds for translation and printing of the source books.

Peggy Oti-Boateng
UNIFEM Consultant
University of Science and Technology, Ghana

Barrie Axtell
IT Consultants, Rugby, UK

Preface

This source book is one of a continuing series which aims to increase awareness of the range of technological options and sources of expertise, as well as indicating the complex nature of designing and successfully implementing technology development and diffusion programmes.

The United Nations Development Fund for Women (UNIFEM) was established in 1976, and is an autonomous body associated since 1984 with the United Nations Development Programme. UNIFEM seeks to free women from under-productive tasks and augment the productivity of their work as a means of accelerating the development process. It does this through funding women's projects which yield direct benefits and through actions directed to ensure that all development policies, plans, programmes and projects take account of the needs of women producers.

In recognition of women's special roles in the production, processing, storage, preparation and marketing of food, UNIFEM initiated in 1985 a Food Cycle Technologies project with the aim of promoting the widespread diffusion of tested technologies to increase the productivity of women's labour in this sector. While global in perspective, the initial phase of the project was implemented in Africa in view of the concern over food security in many countries in the region.

A careful evaluation of the African experience in the final phase of this programme showed that there was a need for key catalytic intervention which would lead to the building of an enabling environment for women's easier access to technologies. This would be an environment where women producers could obtain such information, have the capacity to analyse such information and make technological choices on their own, and acquire credit and training where necessary to enable their purchase and operation of the technology of their choice. This UNIFEM source book series aims to facilitate the building of such an environment.

Introduction

IN MANY PARTS OF THE WORLD it is women who are mainly responsible for the production, processing and selling of foods and this generates the main source of their income. They are involved in two broad types of work: transporting produce either to sell in bulk or retail in a local market, or further processing the food for sale in small shops and stores. Both of these groups face problems which involve packaging.

The women who take produce in bulk to market may suffer financial loss because of spoilage taking place either during long-distance transport or rough handling. Those who produce processed foods for sale are faced with ever greater competition from commercially produced goods. In many countries they may not be permitted to sell their products unless they meet local food laws regarding the contents, packaging and labelling.

Packaging is thus of enormous importance for women producers, and can provide a means to improve incomes by reducing losses, or adding value to a processed food by making the product more competitive in the market.

This source book aims to provide a broad overview for non-technical consultants considering projects in which packaging is involved. It should allow them to make more informed judgements about the problems they face prior to calling upon specialist advice. Such advice is important and a list of relevant institutions and contacts has been included at the end of the book.

Information is provided on the two main applications of packaging: that for containing bulk quantities of produce, and that needed for processed foods in retail packs. The emphasis in this source book, however, is placed on the second area because field experience indicates that this is the area of greatest concern for women producers.

After examining the importance and principles of packaging, the socio-economic aspects of women's involvement in packaging projects are considered. Chapter 2 covers traditional packaging systems, while Chapter 3 examines the use of recycled materials (particularly glass) and newer materials such as plastic for improved packaging. Appropriate small-scale equipment such as fillers, sealers and closing machines is described. The final chapter presents case studies of women who are successfully using some improved packaging technologies.

With some exceptions (egg trays, pottery, paper and woven materials), the production of 'modern' packaging materials is highly complex and expensive. It is therefore not covered in this source book. It is worth noting, however, that recent developments in small-scale plastic vacuum-moulding techniques may offer limited opportunities in some countries.

1
The importance of packaging

THE PREVENTION OF FOOD LOSSES is of vital concern to small-scale producers, and various measures can be applied at all stages between the grower and the consumer in order to reduce wastage, improve food security and generate income and profit.

The use of appropriate packaging is one of these measures and when properly applied can have a dramatic effect, reducing losses and ensuring that products reach the customer in the best possible condition. Appropriate packaging can range from the proper use of containers in which to transport produce to local markets, through to sophisticated systems that can extend the shelf-life of a processed foodstuff for a year or more. Essentially, packaging:

o aims to provide protection from all types of external damaging effects;
o is an integral part of the food-processing chain and helps both producers and consumers to transport, store, sell, purchase and use foods more efficiently;
o is a means of ensuring that the product is delivered to the user in known quantities and in the expected condition for a specified shelf-life;
o is a means of making the food more attractive in order to promote its use and increase sales;
o conveys information to customers about the type of food they are buying, how to prepare it, its shelf-life, and that it conforms to relevant food legislation.

Thus, at its simplest level, packaging contains and protects, while at its most sophisticated it takes on additional roles such as preserving, selling, informing and enhancing the convenience element of the product.

The type of packaging required depends mainly on the nature of the product, the length of time and conditions under which it will be transported and stored before use, the final market for which it is intended and local food laws. If the food is to be consumed near to where it is produced and eaten quickly after processing, little or no packaging may be required. A good example of this is cooked foods wrapped in leaves that are commonly sold on the streets by women. However, if the product is aimed, for example, at a distant export market, the packaging requirements can become extremely complicated. At the point of sale, good packaging and presentation helps to attract customers, and may prove more convenient in use.

Therefore, while packaging is of vital importance everywhere, solutions to problems will differ according to the region or country. There will be variations in economic and cultural circumstances and in the availability of packaging materials, distribution systems, climate, consumer habits and legislation which will affect the choices to be made.

Improvements and changes in packaging have the potential to provide real benefits to a vast number of women. These benefits may come from simply improving the quality of the product they sell in the market, or from adding value to the product by enhancing its appearance and marketability. Often, women producers may try to avoid local food laws by only selling to their friends because their products do not meet with local regulations. In many cases, simple changes such as the design of and the information given on a label,

```
┌─────────────────────────────────────────────────────────────┐
│                       Product name                           │
│                                                              │
│            INGREDIENTS IN ORDER BY WEIGHT                    │
│                                                              │
│    Name and address of maker          Net weight of contents │
└─────────────────────────────────────────────────────────────┘
```

Figure 1. The minimum information that a label should contain

having samples tested or the production place checked, will overcome such constraints. If the appearance of a product can also be enhanced by appropriate packaging at comparatively little extra cost, small producers will be able to compete more effectively against commercial brands.

Principles of packaging

The selection of the appropriate package depends on several basic principles. In order to specify the best choice for a particular use, it is necessary to take into account the type of product, the use for which the packaging is required (bulk, retail, etc.), the duration of storage and distribution (shelf-life), climatic conditions and local availability of materials.

Good packaging protection is particularly important in countries with tropical and humid climates, where food spoilage is more rapid. In fact, a greater level of protection is required than would be necessary in temperate countries, to give a similar storage life.

Regardless of whether the package is a large one (perhaps for distribution to an industrial consumer) or small (for sale to the end user), it has three basic roles:

o to act as a container, enabling the chosen quantity to be handled as a unit without loss, during distribution and storage;

o to protect against squashing, breakage and spoilage during distribution and to

maintain the food in good condition through a planned shelf-life;

o to communicate necessary information about the foodstuff, such as its origin, method of use, weight, quality, or destination.

All these functions are influenced by three basic factors or causes:

o physical damage, including pilferage;
o climatic effects;
o contamination by micro-organisms, insects or foreign matter.

Physical damage

Physical damage and breakage can occur in a number of ways, including vibration, dropping, crushing, squashing or sometimes pilfering. Vibration can seriously affect some processed foods: for example, the volume of powdered products may be reduced through shaking, so making the packet appear half-full; and brittle dried vegetables and snack foods may be broken down to a powder; soft fruits are easily damaged by bruising and after this spoilage is very rapid. Individual wrapping of fruit, combined with packing in the correct outer container, will reduce bruising and prevent contamination spreading from fruit to fruit should this occur.

Retail packs such as plastic bags and bottles need to be packed in outer containers, usually cardboard boxes, to give adequate protection against crushing and breaking. Both the individual container and the outer box must be carefully selected to ensure that they can be stacked safely and so avoid damage during transport.

Unfortunately, pilfering, adulteration and deliberate contamination do occur and result not only in loss, but at worst, damage the good name of the producer who may lose a market as a consequence. Packaging can, to some extent, prevent such deliberate acts. The pilfer-proof bottle cap described in one of the case studies is a good example.

Climatic effects

The damaging effect of moisture is probably the most important factor, and is the principal consideration in protection by packaging when dry products or confectionery are involved. Most dry foods will tend to absorb moisture, the rate depending on the local humidity. This means that greater protection has to be provided in tropical humid countries. Further information on the selection of packaging materials for dry foods will be found in the section on plastics. In some cases, such as sugary fruits and moist fresh foods, the product may tend to dry out, and again the correct wrapping must be used.

Higher temperatures also cause more rapid spoilage. While this is most obvious and critical when dealing with fresh produce, the shelf-life of sealed containers, such as tins or bottles, is reduced in tropical countries. Packaging itself cannot do much to control temperature, but certain steps are possible. Fresh produce should be packed in containers that allow ventilation, and these can be covered with wet leaves or sacks which help to cool the produce. Other simple measures, such as keeping the produce away from direct sunlight and using well-ventilated stores will reduce temperature-related losses.

The effect of air, or more precisely oxygen, is most noticeable in foods high in oils and fats. Oils such as palm oil stored in drums or bottles which have not been completely filled or lack proper closures will become rancid, resulting in loss to the producer. The shelf-life of oily foods such as fish, coconut products or nuts can be extended by packaging that does not allow the entry of air.

Light can cause quality loss through fading of colours, and is also involved in the development of rancidity. For these reasons many products, such as fats or wines and beers, are packed in light-proof containers such as dark-coloured bottles. Often, however, there is a distinct advantage in using transparent packaging in order to let the customer see the product clearly. A balance must be struck between protection and marketing.

Contamination

A major role of packaging is to minimize contamination and prevent the growth of micro-organisms in the product after it has been processed. It does this in two ways:

o by protecting the food from external contamination by dirt, insects and micro-organisms;
o by preventing the development of an environment inside the package in which micro-organisms can grow.

In a source book such as this, it is not feasible to cover these aspects for all types of products in detail. While common examples that demonstrate the protective importance of packaging are included it is recommended that the appropriate specific product source books in the series should be consulted.

The presence of dirt and dust on any food will increase the rate of spoilage, because it carries micro-organisms with it. If dirt or dust is visible, it will also reduce the marketability of the produce. Any form of wrapping will reduce such

CLIMATIC EFFECTS	CONTAMINATION
Temperature	Bacteria
Moisture	Moulds
Air	
Light	Insects
	Mites
	Rodents
	Birds

**Chemical
composition
of product**

PHYSICAL DAMAGE	OTHER FACTORS
Handling	Pilferage
Transport	Price (value)
Stacking	Availability of packaging
Sampling	Customer appeal
Breaking	Legal

Figure 2. Important factors to consider when selecting a packaging material

contamination but, clearly, fully sealed containers are the best.

Certain products, such as fish, are particularly attractive to insects. In the case of fresh fish the main problem is attack by flies, which often lay their eggs in the flesh; boxing and covering should be used. Dried and salted fish attract beetles as well as flies; again, simple covering and wrapping will greatly reduce insect problems. It should be remembered however, that insects are able to eat their way with ease through most paper or plastic wrappings.

Dry foods tend to pick up moisture, and this creates an environment that will encourage the growth of moulds. Some of these moulds, such as *Aspergillus flavus*, produce poisonous toxins; products such as groundnuts or maize are particularly prone to contamination by this mould. Adequate drying, coupled with the selection of a correct packaging material to keep the product dry will extend the shelf-life considerably and reduce the risk of food poisoning.

Short shelf-life processed foods such as meat products, milk, fruit juices or yoghurt will spoil rapidly through the growth of bacteria, yeasts and moulds if they are not properly packed. Hermetic sealing (having a completely airtight seal) of containers will control such growth provided that the product has been properly processed.

Finally, the package often has a marketing role. Good packaging must comply with local food and labelling legislation which may demand a declaration of net weight, producer, type of food and date of expiry. Attractive packaging can help to sell the product as follows:

o creation of a brand image and style of presentation for the food;
o flexibility in the size and design of the containers;
o convenience in handling and distribution.

Health and safety

Health and safety aspects must be borne in mind when considering certain packaging materials. One principal concern involves *printing inks in contact with food*. Many printing inks contain chemicals known to be carcinogenic (that is, they can cause cancer), which can migrate into fatty foodstuffs. The practice of wrapping meats, fish etc. in newspaper or bags made from used office stationery must be deplored.

Certain plastics contain *plasticizers* to make them soft, polythene film being a good example. These plasticizers can migrate into oily foods and very recent research indicates that they may possibly have a role in cases of impaired vision.

The application of *vacuum and gas packaging* should also be avoided unless rigid control procedures are employed. If they are not, the process carries substantial dangers involving the growth of food-poisoning micro-organisms.

When packing in glazed ceramic containers *the use of lead-based glazes must be avoided*. This is particularly important if acid foodstuffs are involved.

Finally, the use of *natural plant and leaf materials* that are not known to be safe when in contact with foods should be avoided.

Types of packaging materials

As mentioned earlier there are two main applications for packaging. The first is for bulk packaging, either in 'shipping' containers or outer cartons, which contain and protect the contents during transport and distribution. Examples include fibreboard cases, crates, barrels, drums, baskets and sacks.

The second is for retail containers, or consumer units. These are packages which protect and advertise the food in convenient quantities for retail sale and home storage (for example, tin cans, glass bottles, rigid or semi-rigid plastic tubs, collapsible tubes, paperboard cartons, plastic bags, sachets and overwraps).

Each of these will be examined in more detail in Chapters 2 and 3, with an emphasis on retail containers which are particularly relevant to small-scale producers.

Constraints to adequate packaging

Small-scale producers, sellers and processors of foods face a number of common problems which are generally more difficult to overcome in African, Asian and Latin American countries:

○ Producers often lack knowledge of the packaging requirements of the particular food they are involved with, and women may find it difficult to gain access to technical advice.
○ The range of improved packaging materials available tends to be limited, which means that often the choice of material must be a compromise.
○ Many packaging materials are imported, which increases their price. Importing involves ordering large quantities and making a capital outlay beyond the financial means of most small businesses. This means that generally a 'middle-person' or importer is involved, leading to even higher prices.
○ Many types of packaging require special equipment to form the package, fill it and close it. Much of this equipment comes from industrialized countries and is often too big, expensive and inflexible for small-scale production. The case studies include examples where local organizations have designed and manufactured more appropriate machinery.

In most situations the 'technically best packaging system' will be expensive, sometimes to an extent where the consumer may not be able to buy the final product. When considering the choice of packaging which could be used by women producers and processors, the following points should be borne in mind to make it as cost-effective as possible:

o Try to standardize packaging as much as possible – so that larger and more economical quantities can be bought.
o Select cost-effective materials.
o Wherever possible, use locally manufactured packaging.
o Use traditional materials whenever possible, where results of comparable quality can be achieved.
o Use re-usable packaging.

Packaged food classification

Food accounts for approximately half of all the packaged products in the world. Few foods are not packaged in some way; even fresh foods sold in the market or at roadside stands will have been packed for transportation from the place of production to the stall. There are three types of packaged foods, namely:

o fresh food;
o partially processed foods;
o fully processed foods.

Fresh food

This includes all fresh vegetables, fruits, fish and meats that are unprocessed except for limited trimming and cleaning. Because such foods are very susceptible to spoilage they should be consumed as soon as possible and handled in a manner that slows the rate of spoilage. This

includes good storage and temperature control.

The main reasons for packaging fresh food relate to the prevention of physical damage, such as bruising and protection from external contamination (insects, dust, etc.), and environmental effects such as drying out and protection from sunlight.

Partially processed foods

Foods with short shelf-lives can be altered by processing in some way in order to slow down spoilage. These include many dairy products and cured meats which have to be kept refrigerated to slow down micro-biological spoilage. These are packaged both to contain the food and to protect it from external contamination.

Fully processed foods

Foods intended for a long shelf-life at room temperature include heat or chemically-treated foods, dried foods, smoked and salted fish and oils that have been refined before packaging.

The selection of a suitable package for any of these products must be based on:

o an accurate knowledge of the product including, for example, its acidity, oil content and its susceptibility to spoilage;
o the types of physical damage that it might meet during transport, distribution and the required shelf-life;
o the climatic conditions under which it is to be transported or stored.

In a book of this size, it is not possible to consider individual products in great detail, but more information is contained in the other books in the Food Cycle Technology series.

Socio-economic considerations

Planning

The majority of African, Asian, and South and Central American food producers, processors, and sellers are women. Food is processed either for home consumption or for commercial purposes, the latter providing a source of income for women who generally have limited access to cash. One particular field of expertise, packaging, usually concerns commercial food processors rather than those providing food for their household. Packaging can reduce losses and increase sales, but on the other hand will also involve paying attention to food laws and will probably increase the costs of a food-processing business. As a result, this area requires careful consideration of business economics and health and safety regulations, as well as the social and cultural concerns of women producers.

Step 1 – Is the new technology commercially viable?

In working out the viability of different options for improving packaging methods, food processors should calculate the following.

Existing profit
Calculate the monthly costs of the business. This should include both the fixed costs (for example, rent, loan payments, the amount put aside for buying or replacing equipment) and the variable costs which change according to the season or amount being produced (for example, materials, labour, transport).

Calculate the monthly total gross income of the business. This should include the total amount of cash received for all the goods sold. If there are no records of money coming in, then estimate the production level and multiply the number of items or weight produced by the price.

Subtract the costs from the gross income in order to get an estimate of the average monthly net income.

Potential profit with new technology
Follow the procedure outlined above, but this time adjust both the cost of materials and the number of sales (which should both be higher) according to the changes resulting from the introduction of new packaging methods. Compare the income earned before and after the use of the new technology. If the increased income outweighs the increase in time, money and effort, then move on to step 2.

Step 2 – Is the new technology appropriate in the context?

Time
Women running commercial food-processing businesses usually have a substantial burden of work. In addition to their business role, they are often responsible for most household work, and even for agricultural or horticultural production as well. Consequently, their commercial work may be seasonal or part-time, thereby leaving sufficient time for their other roles. If the new packaging methods require more work, women may not be able to invest the extra time, and so the new technology may not be socially or economically viable. If, on the other hand, time spent on better packaging can be interwoven with other work tasks, then the new methods may be popular with women. For others, an additional time input will be perceived as worthwhile if the increase in income is sufficient. The viability of new packaging methods must be judged by women themselves since only they can take account of all the aspects of their particular workload and time constraints.

Income and credit

Plainly, those with the lowest incomes can least afford to take financial risks. Buying new packaging materials, and waiting for an interval before increased profits pay back the investment, is obviously more difficult for poorer women. Access to credit is often dependent on where people live (banks and lending institutions may not reach into rural areas), education levels (illiterate people find it harder to borrow money), and on being able to raise collateral. Adopting new packaging methods may only be possible for resource-poor women if they are given assistance with literacy and numeracy, and possibly some kind of group organization skills, in order to secure a loan. Assistance with packaging may only be viable if such economic assistance can also be offered.

Skills/training

Women who have been involved in food processing will already have some packaging knowledge and skills. For instance, existing methods may include wrapping products in leaves, filling sacks, baskets or gourds, or making wooden boxes. Although they are cheap, biodegradable, and often attractive, they offer little protection against moisture, odour, micro-organisms, and insects. This means that the produce cannot be stored for long, thereby forcing the processor to consume or sell quicker than they may wish, to avoid losing the food altogether. Processors may wish to develop their methods further in order to protect the food for longer, but do not always have the necessary knowledge and skills. Adopting new packaging methods is likely to require some technical training. This will only be possible if the women are in a position to invest the time in learning and developing new skills (see above).

In addition to technical training, such as making new containers and learning quality control methods, women may need training or advice on relevant health and safety regulations, business management, marketing, group organization, literacy, numeracy, accounting, and confidence-building. Some skills may not be useful unless combined with others. The adoption of new packaging technology will depend largely upon giving women the opportunity to assess their skill development needs, and responding by offering appropriate advice, assistance and training.

Checklist of socio-economic considerations

Before initiating technical work with women food processors, it is important to assess the need for improvements to packaging. Here are some indications of the kind of questions which should be addressed with those involved during planning:

1. Are there any problems with the existing packaging techniques?
2. Do the producers find that the disadvantages of existing packaging techniques outweigh the advantages?
3. Would more attractive packaging increase the demand for the product?
4. Would the producers be able to meet any extra demand?
5. Would improvements in packaging increase the profit earned by the producers?
6. Would improved packaging make it easier to transport the product?
7. Would improved packaging reduce losses?
8. Do the producers have time for:
   (a) learning about improved techniques?
   (b) collecting materials as necessary?
   (c) making the new packaging?
9. Would the producers have access to the necessary money to pay for the packaging materials?

10. Would resource-poor producers have access to the necessary technical knowledge and skills?
11. Weighing up the likely benefits against the resource constraints, is it worth making the investment of time, money and effort to improve the packaging?
12. Will women have control over the income they earn?

If the answer to the majority of the questions above is 'yes', then a more detailed assessment of possible technical improvements to the packaging methods is probably appropriate. In addition, women should be given the opportunity to make requests for other forms of training and advice (such as group organization, business skills, marketing, obtaining credit, and so on). Plans for training should be founded upon their perception of their own strengths and weaknesses.

Monitoring and evaluation

While the technology is being developed, it is important to monitor progress in order to solve problems, build on developments, and record successes and failures. Monitoring and evaluation should be based on judgements made by the women processors, but within a project it is also useful for staff to appraise their own efforts.

Progress should be measured in areas of interest which may include: level of technical skill; innovative capacity; quality of produce; level of sales; level of income; access to credit; number of processors involved.

At the end of the development phase, when new technology has been either adopted or rejected, it is important to evaluate what has happened. Evaluation tells you whether the technology development is succeeding or failing to meet its objectives. For instance, during and at the end of a project, producers may want to know whether the new packaging has increased sales or not. When success is recognized steps can be taken to consolidate it, and if a failure is spotted, the problem can be identified and dealt with. Evaluations can be used as evidence of good or bad news for others to learn from, and for long-term planning. For example, if produce lasts longer with the new packaging, and more producers become interested in learning the new techniques, then other organizations may support further training work.

Impact should be measured in the same areas of interest considered during monitoring. In addition, the investigation of socio-economic impact should consider who benefits and how additional income or time is distributed between and within households or businesses; who controls the income or time; what the extra money or time is spent on; what positive and negative effects does the new technology have on (a) the individual woman processor; (b) her household; and (c) her community.

2
Traditional food packaging systems

Users of 'traditional' packaging are primarily concerned with reducing wastage and having a container for their food or produce. Their choice of suitable packaging provides protection during a generally short shelf-life and for local distribution. Traditional packaging relies on locally available resources such as bamboo, leaves, rushes, wood and clay.

In many parts of the world agricultural produce is distributed with the minimum of packaging. Traditional packaging materials used for products which do not require protection against moisture include baskets, bales, jute sacks and wooden boxes. These are suitable for commodities such as dried fruits and vegetables, dried or smoked fish, and some fresh fruits and vegetables. Such packages are appropriate for products which are transported in bulk to a central market and then sold loose. Bamboo, calabashes, gourds, earthenware pots and animal skin containers are also used for containing fats, oils and dairy products such as milk, yoghurt and curd, either in bulk or for retail sale. These containers are cheap and have the advantage that they can be used several times, provided they are properly cleaned to minimize contamination.

provide good packaging for products that are quickly consumed. It is also common to find cooked foods of many sorts wrapped in leaves such as banana, bamboo and corn husk, and sold in the market or in the streets by women; dried foods and spices, for example, are commonly sold wrapped in leaves.

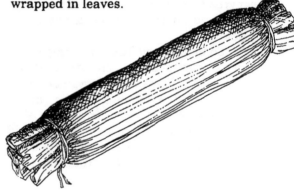

Figure 3. Leaf sausage

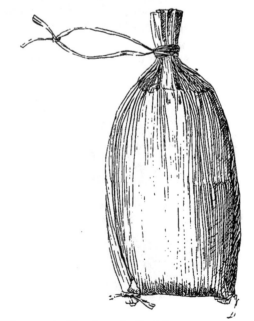

Figure 4. *Peri mula* bottle

Plant materials

Leaves

The leaves of a wide range of tropical plants are used for packaging, either as a direct wrapping or by weaving and forming them into containers and baskets. They are cheap, readily available and

Palm leaves can be skilfully made into containers similar to bottles for holding liquid foods as in the case of the Sri Lankan *peri mula* bottle, used for packaging *kitul* treacle, a sweet palm syrup tasting similar to honey. *Areca* palm leaves are rolled in the shape of a bottle and tied at both ends with strings; the formed shape is filled with sand and left in the sun to dry. The sand is then poured out and the *peri mula* bottle is ready for use.

In the tropics, green coconut palm and papyrus leaves are often woven into bags or baskets for carrying meat, fruits and vegetables.

When using fresh leaves it is important to make sure that they are not contaminated with spider's webs, larvae or pupae which are often common on the undersides of leaves. It is recommended that leaves for wrapping cooked foods should be washed, and the water properly dried off. Dry leaves give better protection than wet ones.

Not all leaves are suitable for wrapping food, as some are poisonous. *Know your leaves.* It is recommended to select only those which are traditionally used for this purpose.

Advantages of using leaves include:

o They are cheap and widely available.
o They offer reasonable protection against dust and flies.
o They are biodegradable.
o In certain circumstances, particularly when catering for middle-class markets, the artistic use of leaves can promote an image of traditional good quality.

Disadvantages are:

o They provide little protection against moisture, odour, micro-organisms and insects and are therefore not suitable for prolonged storage.
o They are not attractive to many consumers as they have an image of a 'poor person's' product.

Plant stems, fronds and fibres

A whole range of plant materials are used for packaging. Common examples include bamboo, jute, rattan, coconut, *kenaf* (*Hibiscus cannabinus*), cotton, papyrus and sisal. In some cases, the fibres are spun to produce a yarn or string which is then to made into bags and baskets for transporting a wide range of materials including grains, legumes, fruits and vegetables. In other cases, bamboo and coconut are made

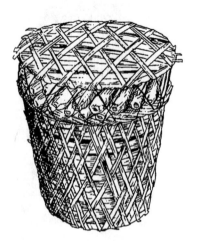

Figure 5. Typical basket weave packaging

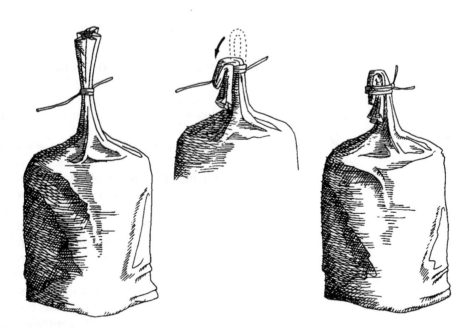

Figure 6. Sack wired at top

into large baskets of different shapes. In many parts of the world most agricultural produce is still brought to the markets packed in such bags and baskets. They all have the advantages of low cost, being made from locally available materials, lightness, flexibility and reasonable strength, making them an attractive packaging material for transporting food in bulk. In addition, their non-slip surface makes them better for stacking than plastic sacks.

Provided that attention is given to the way produce is packed in the baskets, such containers can give good protection from bruising, although containers made out of such plant materials provide little protection against air, moisture, temperature, bacteria and insect attack. They are therefore not used for packaging foods that need to be protected against these hazards during prolonged storage.

Better quality packaging materials can be obtained when vegetable fibres such as jute, cotton, sisal and *kenaf* are indus-

trially woven into sacks. These afford varying degrees of protection and are used for packaging a wide range of foods including cocoa, coffee, rice and grains. The use of a plastic bag inside the sack will provide greater protection against moisture pick-up by dried foods, but should not be used for fresh foods as condensation will promote spoilage.

Natural fibre bags and sacks have certain advantages over the plastic sacks which are increasingly replacing them. They are biodegradable and stack well without slipping, may be re-used several times and in some cases (such as when cotton is used) can be washed with ease. Natural fibre sacks can also be readily repaired by sewing or darning, but they do not provide much protection against moisture and insects unless lined with plastic.

Sacks are normally closed by machine or hand-sewing the top, or by tying with wire, particularly when short-term storage is required.

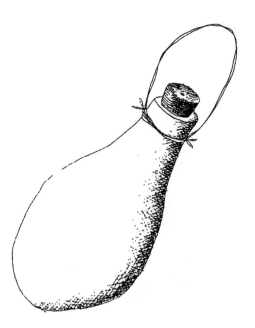

Figure 7. Gourd bottle used for packaging liquid

Vegetable-based containers

Other plant materials that find wide application for storing and transporting water, milk and some dried fruits like dates are gourds and calabashes. These are often closed with a wooden plug, some woven material or with the piece of the gourd which was cut out when the container was made.

Gourd containers are made by carefully cutting the top end off the fruit, scooping out the seeds, washing it out and then drying in the sun for a number of days. Such calabashes have been used in the tropics for thousands of years and when properly closed give better protection against moisture, air and insects than baskets. Gourds and calabashes can be improved by varnishing the outside to make them more moisture-resistant and airtight. They should be washed often and dried in the sun to keep out weevils and to remove the smell of the previous contents.

Figure 8. Applications of earthenware pots

Animal-based containers

Containers made from animal hides – camel, pig, goat, horse, cow, buffalo and antelope – have been used for centuries as containers for storing and transporting water and wine. It is also common to find cassava flour and sugar packed in leather cases and pouches. Leather containers are strong, flexible and can be re-used many times as long as they are washed and dried regularly.

Earthenware

Earthenware containers are used world-wide for storing both liquid and solid foods, such as curd, yoghurt, traditional beers, dried fruits and vegetables, flour, oil and honey. These pots are covered or sealed with ceramic lids, corks, wooden plugs, leaves, waxed cloth or a plastic sheet. Ceramic containers are strong and protect their content against squashing, but they have the disadvantage of breaking easily if dropped or knocked. If used for liquids such as oils, wines and honey, they need to be glazed on the inside, and if well sealed, such products can be stored for more than a year.

Wood

Wood is a strong material used for the construction of many types of boxes and crates for packaging fish, fresh fruits and vegetables. It is also made into barrels, commonly used for storing and transporting liquids such as wine. Wooden containers offer good protection against mechanical damage (breaking, squashing

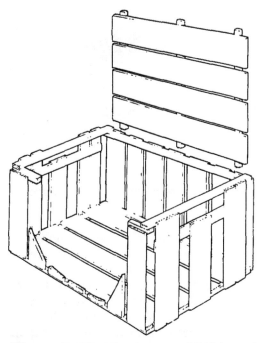

Figure 9. Wooden crate with hinged lid

and crushing) and they also have the advantage of being easily stacked. They can be re-used many times. Care must be taken when using resinous wood that it does not taint the product with the smell or taste of resin.

Wooden boxes can be used either as outer containers for transporting food in bulk or as small packs for retailing products such as tea, confectionery and spices. Such containers give little protection against climatic effects but, when lined with plastic film or aluminium foil and covered, can be made airtight. For example, plywood chests lined with metal foil are widely used for packaging tea, as they are cheap and effective at keeping tea in good condition.

The performance of a wooden container depends largely on the method used to hold the component parts together. Boxes and crates are traditionally made from sawn wood using simple equipment and

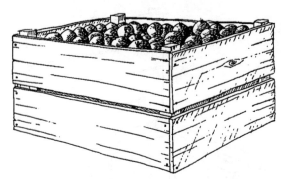

Figure 10. Open crate with stacking corners

methods. This operation will usually require a hand or power saw. The components are then cut to size and hand-made into a box by nailing. For larger-scale production of boxes, however, jigs should be made so that components do not have to be individually measured or placed in position for nailing. Collapsible boxes can also be produced, making them easy to transport before use. The manufacture of barrels, while not requiring expensive tools, is a skilled craft requiring

specialized training and equipment. Damaged wooden containers can often be satisfactorily repaired by renailing or replacing damaged parts with new sections.

The greatest potential for assisting women involved in the distribution and sale of their produce in bulk probably lies in the area of improved organization together with simple advice on how to pack the produce better. Much of the product damage and loss that producers encounter is because of the lack of control they have over the way their produce is handled as it moves to a market. Organizing themselves into groups and transporting in larger quantities can enable them to have greater control over the transport conditions. In addition, simply being certain not to include any bruised or damaged fruits that can spread contamination in a basket, individually wrapping produce in paper, altering the way the produce is packed in the container or including plastic liners in sacks will all help to reduce losses in transport and distribution.

3
New packaging materials and techniques

WITH POPULATION GROWTH and people migrating to towns some distance from where the food is grown, together with the increasing range of non-traditional food products, a wider range of packaging is required. It must be able to withstand transportation hazards, provide longer shelf-life and protect a range of non-traditional products.

In this chapter, possible improvements to traditional methods are discussed, together with the newer forms of packaging such as plastic films. Examples of appropriate small-scale closing and filling equipment are included. While some of the improved technologies described might appear expensive for women producers with small businesses, the case studies show that, despite the high initial investment, good packaging can substantially increase incomes.

With the increasing influence of advertising upon customers, many small food processing enterprises will have to improve the packaging and preservation of their products if they are to survive against competition.

Manufactured packaging is relatively expensive and it is therefore important to select only appropriate packaging materials based on an accurate knowledge of the food to be packed. Consideration should be given, for example, to whether the package will allow moisture to pass through it into a dry food, or whether the product needs to be provided with an airtight seal or protected against light, mechanical shock and damage, or insects. An additional factor which should be borne in mind is whether the packaging will itself react with the food it contains.

The recycling and re-use of packaging materials will be covered in this chapter because it is a common practice in many developing countries. Indeed, re-usable glass is for many women producers the only practical option available. Brief descriptions of closures and closing equipment are provided later in this section.

Paper packaging

Paper is produced in most African, Asian and Latin American countries from wood pulp, banana or papyrus leaves, grasses, rice husks or recycled paper. It is widely used for wrapping commodities such as vegetables, sugar, salt, fish and both cooked and uncooked foods.

As paper easily absorbs water and becomes soft it is not recommended for wrapping fresh foods with a high moisture content meant for prolonged storage.

There are two main types of paper: *kraft paper* and *sulphite paper*. Kraft paper is strong and commonly made into multi-wall paper sacks for packaging powdered foods, flours, cereals, legumes, fruits and dense products such as potatoes. Paper sacks are easy to handle and store but may not be readily available in all countries. *Vegetable parchment* is a specialized paper which has greater oil resistance and wet strength and is therefore used for wrapping oily foods.

Sulphite paper is lighter and weaker and finds use for grocery bags, sweet wrappers, and in laminates. *Greaseproof paper* is a type of sulphite paper that is resistant to oils and fats but loses this property if the paper becomes wet; it is widely used for wrapping fish, meat, dairy products, and baked foods like biscuits and cakes. *Glassine* is a grease-proof paper with more resistance to fats when dry. *Tissue paper* is not resistant to either oil or water and is often used to wrap and protect fruits against dust and bruising.

All papers have negligible moisture or gas barrier properties. They are not heat-sealable unless they are coated or laminated with wax or an overlay of plastic film. They are commonly treated with wax by coating – dry waxing, in which the hot wax penetrates the paper, or wax sizing, in which the wax is added during the preparation of the pulp.

Waxed papers have improved moisture barrier properties, and can be heat-sealed. However, a simple wax coating is easily damaged by folding or by abrasive foods. This can be overcome by laminating the wax between layers of paper and/or polythene. For adequate protection against moisture absorption a separate plastic film liner of sufficient thickness is needed.

Paper boards

Boards are made in a similar way to paper but are thicker and stronger and give better protection against breakage and physical damage. The main characteristics of boards are their thickness, stiffness and ability to bend without cracking. *White board*, which is in fact not always white, is suitable for being in contact with food and is often coated with polythene, polyvinyl chloride (PVC) or wax to make it heat sealable. It makes good outer cartons for cereals, tea, flour, and so on.

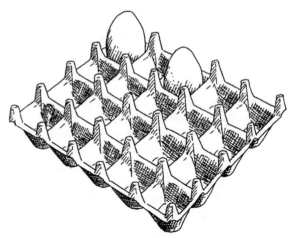

Figure 11. Moulded paper egg tray

Moulded paper pulp trays

Small-scale, labour-intensive paper pulp moulding systems are available in which recycled paper can be moulded into egg trays and a range of shallow dishes and containers. Essentially, the process involves pulping the paper and then forming it using vacuum over a mould. The wet-moulded paper is then removed and dried. Dyes and waxes can be added to the pulp to give packaged products a better appearance and higher resistance to moisture.

Simple equipment has been developed in India that uses a combination of heat and pressure to mould shallow plates and trays from leaves.

Laminated paper board cartons

A number of different types of plastic and paper board laminates are used for packaging sterilized and pasteurized foods such as milk and fruit juices. While cartons of this type, which are often known as 'Tetrapaks', are available in many developing countries, the capital cost of the equipment to form, fill and seal them is high and requires production on a large

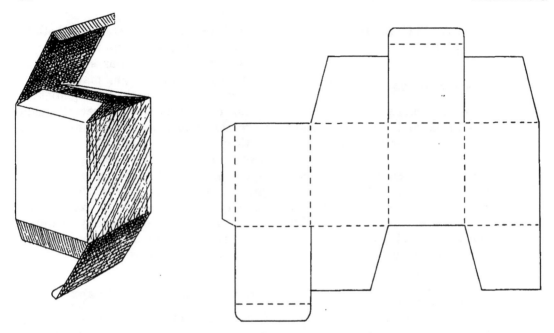

Figure 12. A side-glued carton design

scale. It is therefore likely to be beyond the financial capacity of small-scale women producers.

Fibreboard is made of solid or corrugated board and, if the correct grades are selected for the particular foods and transport conditions, can provide good protection. Fibreboard boxes for fresh fruits and vegetables are usually made with ventilation holes to enable the temperature and atmosphere inside to be controlled. They are commonly used for the large-scale export of fruits and vegetables. Small fibreboard cylinders with plastic or metal caps are commonly used for confectionery and spices while large drums provide a cheap alternative to metal drums; they are used for packaging powders and, when lined with polythene, for fats.

Corrugated board has an outer and inner lining of kraft paper with a central corrugating (or fluting) material. The board is cut into shapes which are assembled before filling. High humidity may cause delamination of the corrugated material, although this can be prevented to some extent by using water-resistant adhesives. Such boxes are mostly used for transporting: the familiar 'cardboard box'. Single sheets of board are used for smaller retail packs. Transfer of moisture from the foodstuff to the box can be prevented by lining with polyethylene film, or greaseproof paper. Such systems are used for packaging frozen products and dairy foods.

Although fibreboard and corrugated board are not usually made on a small scale, it is sometimes possible to produce them by hand using a sharp knife or guillotine. With practice, lines may be scored so that the cardboard will fold into shape without breaking. A typical example is shown in Figure 12. Such boxes can be lined with suitable materials for extra protection and may allow producers to improve the presentation of a product and so increase its marketability. Simple labels can be printed with the business logo to make the box more attractive and advertise the product.

Closing paper-based packaging

While automatic closing systems are commonly used in large industries, hand-closing will be usual for the small-scale sector.

Paper sacks are often closed by machine sewing, sometimes with a tape applied over the stitching. They are also commonly tied with wire or sealed by hand with heavy duty staples.

Fibreboard boxes may be closed using gummed paper, plastic adhesives, tape, staples or glue. The use of glue makes it more difficult to open the box in a way which will permit re-use. Small boxes can be closed more firmly, if necessary, by using self-adhesive tape or glue.

Re-usability

Boxes can be re-used if they are not damaged. If the damage is slight and the containers will not be subjected to further severe hazards it may be possible to make some repairs by taping damaged areas or re-taping faulty seams.

Metal containers

The most widely used metal containers are the tin cans used for meats, fruit juices, and so on. Larger tinplate containers, up to 5 gallons (approximately 22.5 litres) capacity, are used to pack oils and dry products. Coated steel drums of up to 45 gallons (approximately 200 litres) capacity are commonly used for vegetable oils. The inner coating must be of a material that does not react with the oil; tinplate and some types of plastic are commonly used. In recent years, aluminium is being used more and more both as foil for wrapping or in the form of small trays and cans. Metal has a number of advantages as a packaging material as it can provide perfect protection against external contamination. However, metal containers tend to be relatively expensive, particularly when compared with the newer plastic-based packaging which is replacing them. The suitability of the tin can for use in small industries run by women should not be totally excluded, as in countries with a can-making facility it can be cheaper than alternative imported materials such as glass.

Three-piece 'sanitary' cans

Sanitary cans are used for packing a very wide range of products including vegetables, soups, fish, meats and fruits. They are available in various sizes from about 100 grams to 3 kilograms. Different shapes exist, the most common being the cylinder, but flat, oval and square tins are used, particularly for fish. Sanitary cans are made from steel, coated internally with a thin layer of tin and a lacquer or varnish to prevent corrosion, and are

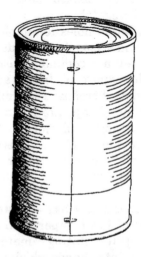

Figure 13. A made-up sanitary can

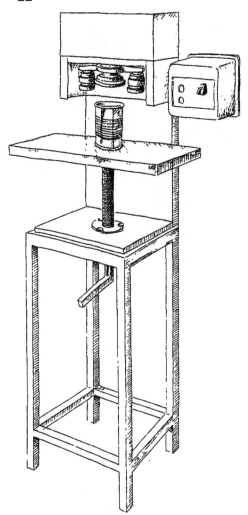

Figure 14. Small electric canning machine

machines and also to 'strip down a can' to make sure that an adequate seal has been made.

The use of sanitary cans can be appropriate at small industry level, depending on the price and availability of alternatives, and provided that specialized technical advice is locally available. It must be stressed, however, that such applications must be restricted to acid products such as fruit juices.

> IF ERRORS OCCUR WHEN CANNING VEGETABLES, MEATS AND FISH, THERE IS A HIGH RISK OF FOOD POISONING WHICH MAY BE FATAL. IT IS NOT RECOMMENDED FOR SMALL-SCALE INDUSTRY.

Larger tinplate containers with capacities from 2 to 20kg are used for products such as dried milk, biscuits and vegetable oils. They may be round or square and have special pouring devices at one end or simply have a press-on lid. They provide excellent protection in humid climates. Such containers are most appropriate for use in many women's projects, as with care they can be re-used several times and are often available second-hand. If second-hand tins are used the various precautions pointed out in the section on recycling *must* be considered.

Steel drums

Drums of 20 to 200 litre capacity are most commonly used for the transport of vegetable oils and fats. When properly coated, or lined with a large plastic bag, they can prove useful for storing products such as fruit purées or chutneys. They provide good protection and are usually strong enough to withstand rough handling. Steel drums are available with various types of closures: with a pouring device or a press-on lid, with or without a screw tightening ring. Those with press-on lids

most suitable for products that require thermal processing – that is, filling, sealing and then cooking in the can, often under pressure.

They are available in two forms: as 'made-up' cans, with the base already in place, and as 'flattened cans' where the user has to seal in both the base and lid. Figure 13 shows a typical made-up can.

Simple hand-operated can-sealing machines are available, as shown in Figure 14. It is most important that producers are trained to set up and adjust such

are very useful for storing and transporting dried foods in bulk, while drums with pouring devices are used for oils. The use of an unlined steel drum for acid fruit juices and products containing a lot of salt is not recommended as corrosion will occur. Because of their strength, steel drums can be re-used many times. They are widely used to transport a range of chemicals and materials such as kerosene or fuel oil. It is imperative that drums that have been used for such materials should not be used for foodstuffs. In many cases, drums that have contained dangerous materials such as pesticides are clearly marked on the outside. Such drums should never be used for food.

Aluminium foil

Aluminium provides an excellent barrier for protecting foods and has the advantage of being heat-resistant. It finds wide use nowadays for wrapping 'fast foods'. It is also widely used for wrapping cheese, meat, vegetables and confectionery. Foil and formed aluminium dishes, often with a cardboard cover (known as composite containers) can be a good solution for women entrepreneurs producing street foods, as they provide a more professional appearance and better protection than leaf wrapping. Aluminium foil is, however, more expensive than traditional alternatives and because it tears easily it is difficult to re-use.

Glass containers

Glass is a very widely used packaging material available in a large range of shapes, sizes and colours of bottles and jars. Provided it is well sealed, a glass container gives excellent protection against external contamination and,

being inert (that is, it cannot corrode), it does not react with the food. Provided care is taken, glass bottles and jars can be hot-filled, and this makes them suitable for the heat processing of juices, jams and pickles. Some types, such as beer or soft drink bottles, can withstand considerable internal pressure. Clear bottles help to display the contents, and green and brown bottles can offer protection against light when it is needed. They are strong, which enables stacking without damage, and the contents can be clearly seen by customers, possibly adding value to the product. In addition, they have the great advantage of being re-usable.

Glass containers have certain disadvantages, such as their weight, which adds to transport costs, their cost, and their breakability when not carefully handled. In addition, there is always a risk of glass splinters finding their way into the food.

Re-use of glass containers

Glass containers, provided they are in good condition, can be re-used if suitable new caps are found; indeed, many large food industries rely on the efficient return and re-use of their bottles. This is particularly true of breweries and soft drink manufacturers.

Great care must be taken to ensure that the bottles have not been used for any non-food purpose. Such practice is potentially very dangerous if, for example, they have been used for pesticides, but other materials such as kerosene can taint the food. Careful visual inspection and smelling must be carried out, and any chipped, damaged or suspect bottles rejected.

After inspection the bottles must be thoroughly cleaned and sterilized. This is best done by washing with a mild cleaning agent (for example, caustic soda, ranging from 0.5 to 3 per cent concentration)

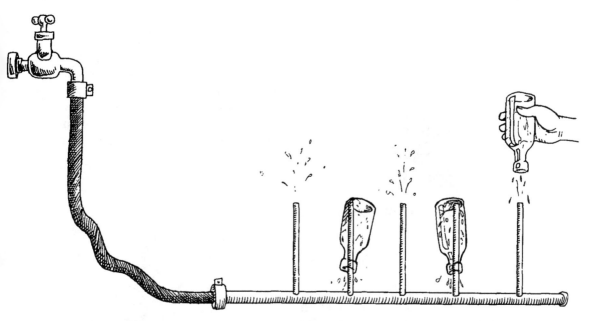

Figure 15. Simple bottle rinsing equipment

usually together with some detergent to ensure the removal of dust, grease and old labels.

The containers must be thoroughly rinsed to get rid of any excess detergent; a simple rinsing apparatus has been developed and found useful.

Bottles to be re-used for packaging of food must be sterilized to eliminate or reduce any infection by micro-organisms. Sterilization can also be done by boiling the jars and bottles in a large container with the water fully covering the bottles, or by steaming them.

Caps and closures

Small production units that rely on glass for packaging may encounter problems related to closing or sealing the bottle. This is the critical step, as the performance of the bottle is dependent on the closure used. Other production operations such as cleaning, filling and labelling are normally carried out by hand, but in many cases special equipment is required to fit the bottle cap or closure. In many countries the special types of caps required are unavailable or difficult to acquire, or have to be purchased in very large quantities which makes the initial outlay prohibitively high.

While ideally the correct new cap should always be used to seal a bottle, many small-scale producers use simpler, cheaper but less effective methods. These are normally used for home-bottling of foods that will be consumed within a short time. Common methods include:

o plastic film or waxed paper, tied or wrapped over the mouth of the bottle and held in place with a rubber band;
o edible oil or fat poured on top of products such as tomato paste;
o paper or plastic, sterilized by dipping it in alcohol and put on top of the product immediately after filling; damp cellophane is then stretched over the top of

Figure 16. Jar sealed with plastic film tied to neck

the jar and this shrinks when dry to form a good seal;

o a round piece of cloth sterilized in boiling water, dried and dipped into melted candle wax, then quickly tied over the neck of the jar and held in place by a string;

o corks or wooden stoppers, sealed with molten wax, give an airtight seal.

However, when producing for a formal market sector, there are certain quality control requirements. This means that more 'professional' closures which provide better protection against contamination must be used.

There are five basic types of bottle necks and closure systems. These will be dealt with individually below, together with examples of simple equipment available to apply caps on a small scale.

Crown caps

Crown caps are applied by pressure to the top of the bottle and seal hermetically onto a glass ring built into the bottle neck. They are widely used for capping beer and fruit drink bottles. Several grades exist that are designed for different products, for example those of high acidity. When opened the hermetic seal is broken and the caps cannot be refitted. They are ideally used for products that are completely consumed immediately after opening. Crown caps cannot be fitted by hand, but small manual machines are available (see, for example, Figure 17). Crown caps are cheap, easy to apply and provide a hermetic seal; they are, however, not reusable and can corrode in humid climates.

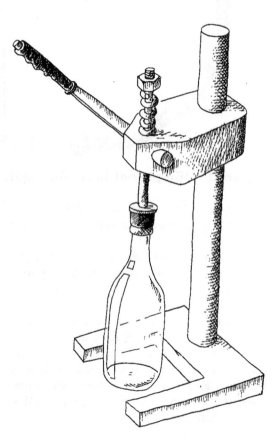

Figure 17. Hand operated crown corking (capping) machine

Roll-on capping

Bottles to which this type of cap are applied have a simple continuous thread built into the neck. Typical examples are spirit bottles, larger 'dilute-to-taste' fruit drink packs and certain jars for jams and pickles. These caps have a cardboard,

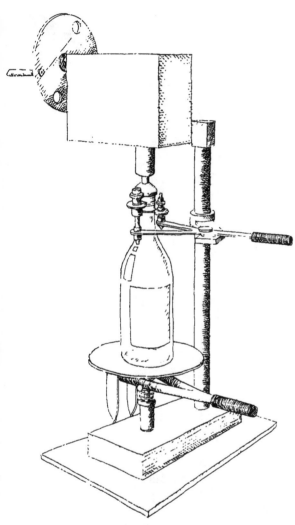

Figure 18. ROPP capping machine

protection. Such shrink-rings are often supplied submerged in liquid and, when taken out and put over the cap and bottle-neck, they dry out and shrink tightly onto the pack.

A slightly more sophisticated cap in-cludes an integral pilfer-proof seal. These are known as 'roll-on pilfer-proof' (ROPP) and are commonly used on spirit bottles. They are very similar to the unthreaded caps described above, except that a sec-ond wheel in the capping machine folds the bottom of the cap over a ring built into the bottleneck. This weakens the bottom of the cap so when it is unscrewed, it breaks away from the main body of the cap and leaves a small ring fixed to the bottle. Such caps are particularly useful for higher-value products, which may be susceptible to pilfering or adulteration.

Both plastic and metal versions are available of all three caps described above.

cork or plastic inner liner. There are three basic types.

The simplest is purchased already threaded and can be readily applied by hand. Slightly more complicated are caps which are bought without a thread and resemble a cup. These are put over the bottleneck and a wheel on the capping machine forces the metal of the cap into the pre-formed thread of the glass bottle. Closures of this type are not pilfer-proof, but small coloured plastic shrink-rings can be purchased to give the pack added

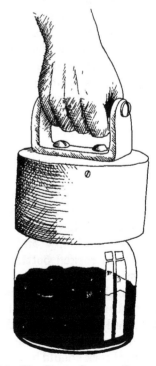

Figure 19. Push-on jar sealer

Push-on lids

This type of closure, often known by its tradename 'Omnia', gives an airtight seal and is commonly used in capping bottles where a vacuum forms after hot filling, such as with jams. These caps are fitted to jars of various sizes containing a wide range of food products.

Simple manual equipment is available which pushes the cap over the neck of the jar and 'crimps' it onto the glass ring built into the neck to provide a firm seal.

Twist-on-twist-off closures

The jars for this type of closure are manufactured with a different thread design. Caps are bought pre-formed and generally contain a rubber or soft plastic seal inside. They can be applied by twisting them on by hand and in the process the top of the glass neck forms an airtight seal against the lid. Caps of this type can be opened and closed several times and are ideal for products that are not consumed all at once. They are made of plastic or lacquered metal and are commonly used on bottles containing jams, pickles, sauces and mayonnaise.

Corking

Corks are used most commonly to seal wine bottles but, in many countries in Africa, Asia and Latin America, other products such as honey and cooking oil can be seen in corked bottles. In recent years plastic corks have increasingly replaced natural ones. Plastic corks can be used more than once but natural corks should if at all possible be used only once. Small hand-corking machines are available. Natural cork should be soaked in hot water before use.

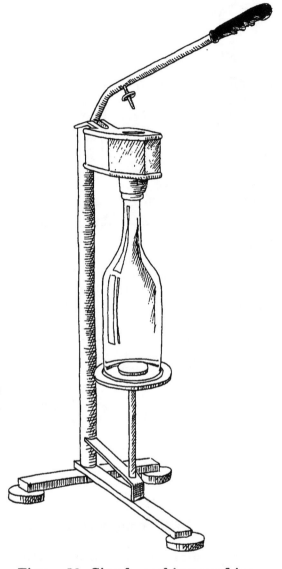

Figure 20. Simple corking machine

Plastics

The phenomenal growth in the range and application of different types of plastic materials has greatly widened the range of packaging available for food products. While a number of types of plastics are now available for containing and wrapping different foods, many of them are, as yet, either unavailable or very difficult to find in African, Asian and Latin American countries.

The basic polymer materials used to make plastics are produced by large chemical companies, with the conversion of these materials into sheets, films and containers being carried out on a smaller scale.

Plastics have a number of advantages over other materials:

o They can be rigid or flexible.
o They are available in a range of thicknesses.
o They have good wet and dry strength and are comparatively chemically inert.
o They provide a good barrier against moisture and air.
o They can be heat-sealed and airtight, or hermetic packaging is possible.
o Flexible types fit closely to the shape of the food, thereby wasting little space during storage and distribution.
o They are light in weight and convenient to use.
o They are generally cheaper than alternatives such as tin and glass.
o They have good sales appeal.

A wide range of plastic materials with different qualities regarding resistance to physical shock, light, heat, moisture and air is produced by varying the product thickness, and by combining different kinds of plastic in layers. This last type are known as co-polymers and laminates. They can also be produced in fibre form for weaving into bags and sacks which are much more durable than vegetable or animal based materials. Plastics have a great environmental disadvantage in that most are not biodegradable.

The following section will examine only the most common types of plastic packaging likely to be available to small-scale producers. It is strongly recommended that technical advice be sought if plastic is being considered for use as a packaging material and care must be taken to ensure that only food-grade types are used.

Polyethylene films

There are two main types of polyethylene: low density and high density.

Low-density polyethylene (LDPE), commonly known as polythene, is probably the most widely used packaging film owing to its versatility and low cost. It can be extruded into film, or used as a coating on paper, aluminium foil or cellulose film.

Polythene bags are used extensively for packaging all kinds of dry and refined foods at home and in the markets in developing countries. As has been mentioned, a polythene film lining in a 'traditional' package can add substantial protection against uptake of water vapour.

Polythene bags need to be used with care because different types of food require different storage characteristics. Certain conditions, such as sweating, could affect hot pastry foods or breads: these foods must be cooled down before packaging.

Low-density polyethylene is heat-sealable and provides a reasonable barrier to moisture. It is, however, very permeable to gases and sensitive to oily products.

High-density polyethylene (HDPE) is thicker, stronger and less flexible and has lower permeability to moisture and gases. HDPE is commonly used in plastic sacks.

Cellulose films

Plain cellulose is a glossy, transparent film made by chemically treating sulphite paper pulp. It is odourless, tasteless and biodegradable after approximately one

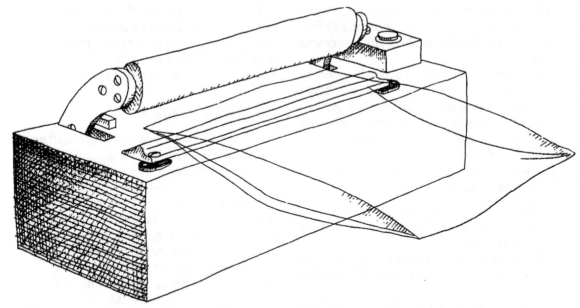

Figure 21. Jaw-type heat sealer

hundred days. It is also tough and puncture-resistant, but tears easily. Although very suitable for twist-wrapping sweets, for example, its disadvantage is that it is not heat-sealable and therefore has limited use. It provides better protection against moisture or air than polythene.

When coated with a lacquer, cellulose film becomes heat-sealable, and this material is called *cellophane*. A wide range of cellophane/paper/foil/plastic film laminates are produced for special purposes. The large-scale use of cellophane is diminishing, but it can be useful for small-scale users because of its heat-sealing property.

Polypropylene films

There are different types of polypropylene films which can be used instead of polythene and cellophane. They provide greater protection than polythene against moisture and air and the use of polypropylene is recommended for foods that may take up moisture or be susceptible to

air. Polypropylene is an attractive glossy packaging material that is considered to have high consumer appeal.

Other plastic films

Polyester is a very strong, transparent, glossy film which has good moisture and gas barrier properties. It is flexible over a wide temperature range and is used for both films and semi-rigid containers.

Uncoated polyvinylidene chloride (PVDC) film is not widely available in some countries. It has very good moisture, odour and gas barrier properties, is fat-resistant and does not melt in contact with hot fats; this makes it suitable for wrapping poultry, ham, 'freezer-to-oven' foods and for the in-store wrapping of cheese. It can be heat-sealed. Tubular forms are used as sausage skins.

More and more commonly, films of the type described above are being used in sheet rather than made-up bag form. Such sheets are used in what are known as form-fill seal machines. Here, a roll of

increasingly replacing glass and metal containers. They have a number of advantages:

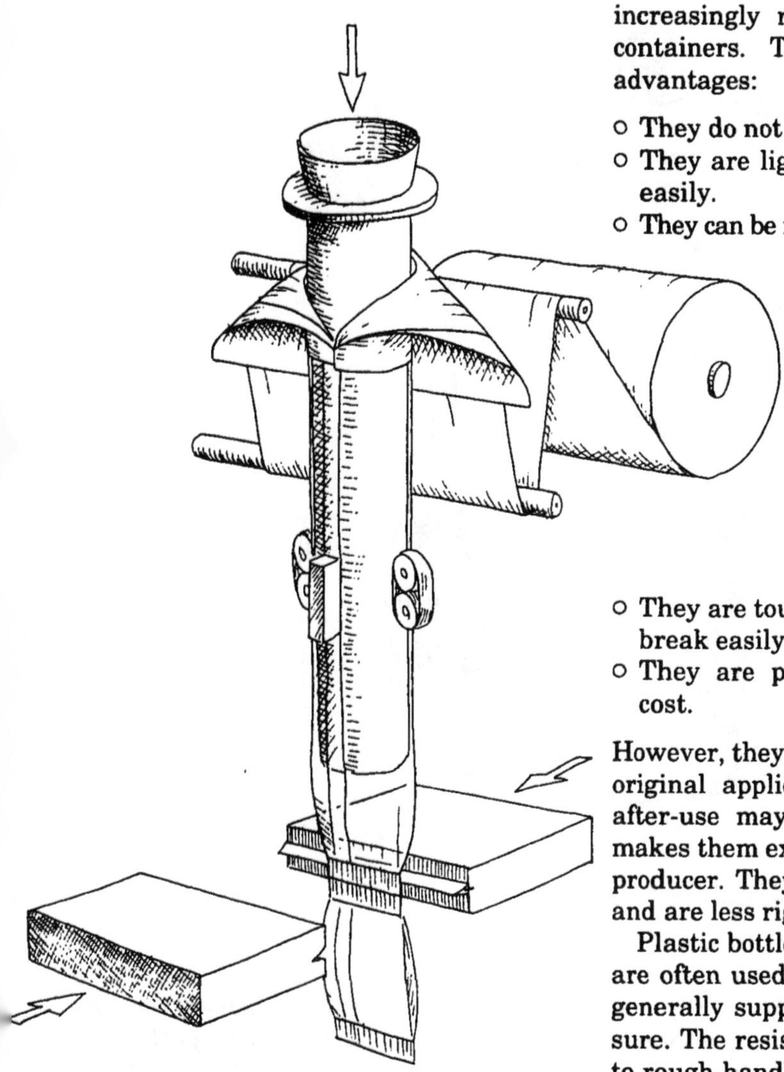

○ They do not corrode.
○ They are light and can be transported easily.
○ They can be moulded into various shapes.

○ They are tough, easy to seal and do not break easily.
○ They are produced at relatively low cost.

However, they are rarely re-used for their original application (although domestic after-use may be important), and this makes them expensive for the small-scale producer. They have low heat-resistance and are less rigid than metal or glass.

Plastic bottles of up to 4 litres capacity are often used for vegetable oils and are generally supplied with a leak-proof closure. The resistance of plastic containers to rough handling depends upon the material (type of polymer) used. Polyvinyl chloride (PVC) bottles, for example, are of low strength and cannot withstand the pressure of carbonation. They are therefore only used for oil, fruit juices, squashes and concentrates.

Bottles are often made from low-density polyethylene if they need to be squeezed. High-density polyethylene is used if a rigid bottle is required and transparency is not essential, while polyvinyl chloride (PVC) is used where transparency and chemical resistance are

Figure 22. Form-fill mechanism

film is formed into a tube, heat-sealed at the bottom, filled with the product and heat-sealed at the top.

A simple jaw-type heat sealer and a form-fill mechanism are shown in Figures 21 and 22.

Rigid containers

Plastic containers such as jars, bottles, boxes, tubs, large drums and trays are

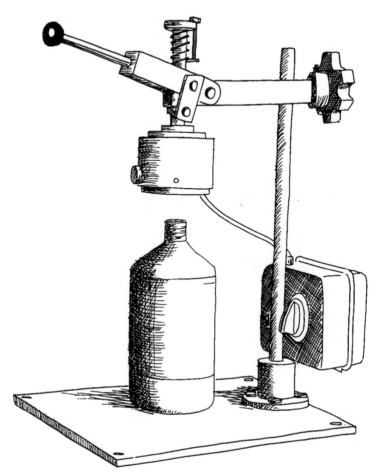

Figure 23. Electric sealer for applying foil lids

important, for example for use with vegetable oils. Polyethylene terephthalate (PET) bottles are particularly important for carbonated beverages.

Jars are usually made of the more rigid plastics and used, especially in small sizes, for cosmetic and toiletry products, but can be used for food products where hot-filling is not required. Wide-mouthed moulded tubs and pails, made of polypropylene or high-density polyethylene in sizes from 1 to 25 litres or more, are suitable for both non-food and food products. Still larger containers, drums and barrels up to 200 litres, are made of high-density polyethylene.

Small white cup-shaped plastic pots are becoming increasingly available. Two types of closure exist: a small plastic push-on lid and a heat-sealed aluminium foil laminate. The latter, which gives a good leak-proof, airtight seal, provides a useful solution to packaging a range of goods including dry foods, yoghurt, jams, pickles and drinks. Heat-sealed lids may be applied with a household iron or by using a special small machine, as shown in Figure 23.

Summary

The selection of a package for a particular foodstuff in a particular situation depends on a range of factors, including the role of the package, the climate, packaging material availability, the market for which it is intended, and the nature of the particular commodity to be packed. Table 1 summarizes the types of protection given by selected packaging materials and the various options that might be considered for different food groups.

Table 1. Protection offered by selected packaging materials if properly sealed

Type of packaging	Protection given to the food against							
	Puncture, crush, etc.	Sunlight	Air	Moisture	Odour	Insects	Rodents	Micro-organisms
Cans	ooo	ooo	ooo	ooo	ooo	ooo	ooo	ooo
Glass (bottle, jar)	ooo–oo	ooo (if coloured)	ooo	ooo	ooo	ooo	ooo	ooo
Paper – Sack	o	oo	o	oo	o	o	o	oo
– Bag	o	oo	o	o	o	o	o	o
Cardboard	oo	ooo	o	o	o	o	o	oo
Wood (Box)	ooo	ooo	o	o	o	o	o	oo
Pottery	ooo–oo	ooo	ooo	ooo	ooo	ooo	ooo	ooo
Foil	o	ooo	ooo	ooo	ooo	oo	o	oo
Plastic films	o	o	ooo	ooo–oo	ooo–oo	o	o	oo
Plastic tubs	o	oo	ooo	ooo	ooo	oo	o	oo

ooo = High
oo = Medium
o = Low

4
Case Studies

Packaging *kitul* treacle, Sri Lanka

THE *KITUL* PALM has many uses in Sri Lanka: the leaves for fodder, the wood for fires and, most importantly, the sap, tapped from the flowers to make *kitul* treacle. *Kitul* treacle manufacture is a traditional rural craft in the country and an important income-generating activity for women.

The sap is collected by tapping the flowers and then, after the addition of a little lime to slow down fermentation, it is slowly concentrated by boiling over a low fire in a smoky kitchen. The treacle thus develops a pleasant smoky flavour. The final sugar concentration must be above 72° Brix to prevent secondary fermentation.

The finished product may still be seen packed in traditional *peri mula* bottles that are made, with great skill, from the leaves of the *Areca* palm. It is now, however, more common for it to be sold in second-hand glass bottles.

The traditional process and packaging have limitations. The sap often starts to ferment, with a consequent loss of yield and the development of 'acid' off-flavours. The final ending-point after boiling is critical: too low and fermentation occurs, too high and the producer loses volume and hence income. Additionally, as *kitul* treacle is a high-value product, consumers are very concerned about adulteration with brown sugar. Indeed, this is very common, and entrepreneurs buying pure treacle from women producers often do adulterate it in this way.

In 1985, research carried out in the capital, Colombo, suggested that a good urban and possible export market demand existed for pure, high-quality treacle. A project was thus set up to meet this demand. The Industrial Development Board (IDB) organized producers into societies and taught improved techniques in which the fresh sap was immediately boiled down and the final sugar content controlled by the use of a refractometer (an instrument use to measure sugar level). After filtration the treacle was hot-filled into 26oz (750ml) bottles fitted with roll-on pilfer-proof caps (ROPP), in turn fitted by a simple, low-cost machine developed by the IDB.

The improved technology made a considerable impact on the marketability of *kitul* treacle. When quality is improved, consumers can have confidence in the product and better prices can be obtained by the producers. The impact of the new process on the women involved is somewhat less obvious. They have now moved their work from their own homes to a village community centre. It has been suggested that it would be better for the group to continue to boil down the syrup at home and simply to use the centre for blending, quality control checks and packaging.

Notes

○ Centralized, controlled production with quality control mechanisms improves the product.
○ Pilfer-proof packaging gains consumer confidence.
○ Centralized processing and packaging may help only a few members of the

community and have a negative effect on others.

o More data needed on rural women's time constraints and the advantages and disadvantages of home versus centralized working.

Yoghurt packaging, Sri Lanka

There is a long tradition of making a yoghurt-like product called curd in Sri Lanka. The curd is made from buffalo milk which is very high in fat. The product is thick, and stands up well to the tropical climatic conditions in the country. Over recent years, however, there has been a growing demand for Northern-style cow's milk yoghurt, particularly from middle-class urban consumers.

In 1986, the Integrated Development Programme for the town of Hambantota in the south of the island reacted to requests to find ways of processing excess milk in the area by investigating yoghurt production. At that time all such production was handled by one or two very large factories in the capital and there were no small rural plants.

With assistance from a visiting food technologist, a simple, safe, low-cost production system was developed. The only major pieces of equipment needed were a refrigerator, which is common in many homes, and a heat-sealer. A number of women entrepreneurs were assisted in setting up their own small-scale yoghurt-producing businesses.

The initial packaging used was a white plastic yoghurt cup which had recently become available in Sri Lanka, fitted with a heat-sealed imported aluminium foil/laminate lid. This provides a high-quality seal and near-perfect protection from contamination by external micro-organisms, a serious problem which can result in food poisoning. Cleanliness is therefore essential at all stages. A small machine was identified for heat-sealing the lids to the pots and this machine is shown in the section on packaging machines (see page 31).

In 1987, however, producers began to reject the heat-sealed lids and move to a less perfect, push-on lid which had suddenly begun to be produced in the country. Producers stated that they preferred this lid as it saved them buying a special heat-sealer and was the same type being used by the bigger producers.

In 1989, during a project evaluation, it was noted that a number of small producers were still operating and that the demand for the products was strong.

Notes

o Sudden availability of yoghurt cups enabled the packaging of cow's milk yoghurt to take place.
o The producers were more concerned that their product looked similar to the large-scale competitors than that it was properly protected.
o Difficulties in obtaining imported heat-sealable aluminium laminate may have contributed to packaging change.

Packaging of tea, Peru

Herbal infusions are traditionally used in Peru as tea. In the Andean region many people grow small quantities of chamomile at the edges of their field and a substantial amount is sold in local markets. In the early 1980s a local entrepreneur realized that there was potential for packaging herbal teas in the form of teabags, but did not have a locally available drying or packaging technology.

The Yerfil company started as a very small business, and in the early days the owner and his wife cut out, filled with a teaspoon and heat-sealed by hand each teabag. This was an extremely slow and laborious process but nevertheless allowed the company to start. As demand increased it was realized that this labour-intensive method was totally uneconomic, and a small, second-hand automatic tea-bagging machine was purchased. These machines can produce 120 bags per minute.

The company has now grown substantially and buys a wide variety of herbs from small producers in Peru. Two bagging machines, including a large new unit, work all day and carry out contract packaging for other companies.

This industry, while owned and managed by a man, has provided up to 25 much-needed jobs for poor women in the urban slum areas around the factory.

While the cost of the automatic packaging machine appears very high, an analysis of the company's profits indicate that some 80 per cent of its profits arise from the packaging operation and not from the drying or growing of herbs. The packaging machine is therefore the heart of the business.

Note

o In the right situation, more sophisticated packaging equipment can result in greater profitability and job creation for women.

Cashew nut packaging, Honduras

In the early 1980s, Pueblo a Pueblo, an NGO based in Houston, Texas, responded to the request made by poor farmers around Chuloteca in the south of Honduras for assistance in processing and marketing cashew nuts, which had been cultivated on a large scale as a result of the government of Honduras agricultural promotion policy.

Pueblo a Pueblo, having been previously involved in selling handicrafts from Honduras, carried out research which showed a possible market for cashew nuts in 'alternative' shops in the USA. The Institute of Nutrition for Central America and Panama (INCAP) visited the farmers and gave advice which eventually led to the setting up of a production unit. In addition, a second product, the dried candied cashew fruit, was identified as having export potential.

Early in the project, both nuts and dried fruit were packed in heat-sealed polythene bags. These did not give adequate protection, however, against spoilage, moisture pick-up, mould growth and the puncturing of the plastic bags by the sharp edges of the nuts leading to post-harvest loss.

Pueblo a Pueblo then helped the producers change to pre-printed heat-sealable cellophane bags, which overcame many of the problems.

However, in 1989, new problems arose with moth infestation, which was traced to two causes. The first was the design of the heat-sealer jaws which made vertical seals. It appeared that this may have allowed tiny larvae to enter and develop into adult moths. Secondly, infestation was occurring in the store. The problem has since been resolved by obtaining a more suitable heat-sealer and improving the storage system. The products are placed in large plastic bags which are then stored in cardboard drums with a lid which gives an airtight seal. Cleanliness and management of the store has been improved.

By 1990, the size of the women's co-operative had increased to between 60 and 70 people, and export sales were estimated at 500kg per annum. Five more women's groups of 50 members each were planned.

This is a clear demonstration of improvement in the socio-economic status of rural women brought about by a co-ordinated effort to improve packaging and storage techniques and preparation of goods for distribution retailing and export, thereby ensuring safe delivery to the consumer in sound condition. The aim of maximizing sales, and hence profit, has thus been achieved.

Notes

o Use of heat-sealable cellophane and correct heat-sealing equipment solved the problems of spoilage and infestation.
o With appropriate support, women producer groups can enter sophisticated Northern markets.
o Aggressive marketing by the NGO's North American team is an important aspect of the enterprise's success.

Fruit juice and jam packaging, Ghana

In the early 1950s, when there were very few established industries in Ghana and most things were imported, a young home economist decided to produce home-made jams for friends. Jam was eaten by many middle-class families who paid a premium for a luxury imported item. With increasing demand from her friends and others, she realized there was a market for her products and decided to increase production from one to two saucepans per day. She packed the jam in second-hand imported jamjars (bought from collectors), with plastic film closures held in place by a rubber band and a handwritten label which stated the

date of manufacture and the fruits used. The simple packaging coupled with a label helped to advertise her product, and within a year she had increased production tenfold. She began actively to market from door to door.

By 1960, she had progressed to a cottage industry using imported bottle caps, both coated twist-on-twist-off and Omnia metal lids, applied by the use of simple manually operated machinery. She employed two family members to help her meet production demands and reinvested her profit in the business. By 1970 she had increased her range of products, expanding into the production of fruit juices and cordials packed in beer bottles closed with crown caps, and was the first entrepreneur to process and can both cream of palm fruits and palm oil for export.

As consumer tastes developed, she improved her processing and packaging techniques by using imported bottles with lids, semi-automatic filling machines, and attractive printed labels. All these had to conform to local and international food legislation and the products were just as competitive as those made by the large state-owned industries. Her standard of packaging improved gradually, as did her knowledge of the markets both actual and potential, making it possible for her to move into the tourist and international markets.

In 1975, she registered the business as a limited company producing a variety of products, and employing over 20 women of whom two were food scientists. She continues to carry out research on packaging and to keep abreast of modern packaging techniques. Her pioneering role in food processing and packaging has earned her the reputation of being a first-class woman entrepreneur. She also runs training programmes for rural women in food processing and packaging.

Notes

o The business started by using simple second-hand packaging materials.

o As the business became more profitable, the entrepreneur made use of improved packaging.

o She improved standards of packaging to meet consumer sophistication and demand.

o Profits were re-invested, and this helped to expand production.

APPENDIX

Alternative trading organizations

THE OBJECTIVE of alternative trading organizations is to promote fair trading for producers in developing countries. Several of these organizations provide technical and marketing assistance to community-based enterprises and will answer technical queries. Individual organizations might have particular geographical and institutional boundaries of operation.

Europe

Alternative Handel
P.O. Box 7053 Hom, 0306 Oslo 3, NORWAY.

Artimo Rwanda V.Z.W
Rue Thys-Straat 6–8, 1150 Brussels, BELGIUM. Tel: 02 770 25 02

Centre for the promotion of imports from developing countries
P.O. Box 30009, 3001 DA Rotterdam, THE NETHERLANDS. Tel: 010–130787, Telex: 27151

Dritte-Welt-Laeden team
Rawiestrasse 5, Postfach 4006, D 4500 Osnabruck/FR, GERMANY. Tel: 0541 70 74 01

EZA (Co-operation in development with the Third World)
A-5028 Salzburg, Lengfelden 169, AUSTRIA. Tel: 6222 52178, Telex: 63 142 RK ELIX A

Federation for the development of utilitarian handcrafts
c/o D. Bouchart, 17 Rue Campagne Premiere, 75014 Paris, FRANCE.

GEPA
Talstrasse 20, 5830 Schwelm, GERMANY. Tel: 02125/10967, Cable: GEPA D-5830Schwelm

Oxfam Trading
Murdock Road, Bicester, Oxon OX6 7RF, UK. Tel: 018692 45011, Telex: 83610

Traidcraft Exchange
Kingsway, Gateshead NE11 0NE, UK. Tel: 0191 487 3191, Telex: 537681

Twin Trading
345 Goswell Road, London EC1V 7JT, UK. Tel: 0171 837 8222, Telex: 264825

North America

Bridgehead Trading
54 Jackman Avenue, Toronto, Ontario M4K 2X5, CANADA. Tel: 416 463 0618, Telex: 06–22199

Floresta
10855 Sorrento Valley Rd, Suite 5, San Diego, California 92122, USA.

Friends of the Third World
Wayne Street, Ft. Wayne, Indiana 46802, USA. Tel: 219 422 6821

Pueblo a Pueblo
1616 Montrose Boulevard, Houston, Texas 77006, USA.

Packaging research institutes

These are mainly private research institutes interested in international exchange of
experience and knowledge in packaging technology, education and training of packaging specialists, international standardization of packaging and marketing. They might
need to charge for their assistance.

Asia

Asian Packaging Federation
c/o Hapan Packaging Institute, Honshu Building, 2–5 chome, Ginza Higashi, Chou-ku,
Tokyo, JAPAN.

China Packaging Institute
62 Sining South Road, T'aipei, Taiwan, REPUBLIC OF CHINA.

Hong Kong Productivity Centre
Rooms 512–516, Gloucester Building, Des Voeux Road c, P.O. Box 16132, HONG KONG.

Indian Institute of Packaging
H-24 Green Park Extension, New Delhi-16, INDIA.

Korea Packaging Institute
Daewan Building 513, 111 Hap-Dong, Suh Dae Mun-Ku, Seoul, KOREA.

Packaging Institute of the Philippines
Room 207 Far East Building, Buendia Avenue, Makati, Rizal, PHILIPPINES.

Thailand Industrial Product Design Centre
Department of Industrial Promotion, Ministry of Industry, Rama VI Road, Phyathai,
Bangkok, THAILAND.

Australia

The National Materials Handling Bureau
105–115 Delhi Road, North Ryde, NSW 2113.

The National Packaging Association of Australia
Manufacturers House, 370 St. Kilda Road, Melbourne 3004.

Europe

Agromisa
P.O. Box 41, 6700 AA Wageningen, THE NETHERLANDS.

Beratungsstelle für Seemassige Verpackung
Hamburg 36, Bleichenbrucke 10, Z.415, GERMANY.

Institut for Lebensmitteltechnologie und Verpackung
8000 Munich 54, Schragenhofstrasse 35, GERMANY.

Institute TNO for Packaging Research
Schoemakerstraat 97, Delft, THE NETHERLANDS.

Intermediate Technology
Myson House, Railway Terrace, Rugby, Warwickshire CV21 3HT, UK.

International Packaging Consultants
Kirvuntie 35A, SF-02140 Espoo, FINLAND.

Laboratoire General pour Emballages
105 Boulevard Suchet, Paris 16e, FRANCE.

Natural Resources Institute
Central Avenue, Chatham Maritime, Chatham, Kent ME4 4TB, UK.

Norwegian Agricultural Institute for Food Packaging
Bks 64, Vollebekk, pr. Oslo, NORWAY.

Norwegian Pulp and Paper Research Institute
Post Box 250, Vinderen – Oslo, NORWAY.

Osterr. Institut für Verpackungswesen
Franz Klein-Gasse 1, A-1190 Vienna, AUSTRIA.

Packaging Industries Research Association
Randalls Road, Leatherhead, Surrey, UK.

Sprenger Institut
Haagweg 6, 6708 PM Wageningen, THE NETHERLANDS.

Stichting Verpakkingsontwekkeling Nederland
Parkstraat 18, The Hague, THE NETHERLANDS.

Swedish Packaging Research Instutute
Elektravagen 53, Box 42054, Stockholm 42, SWEDEN.

TOOL
Sarphatistraat 650, 1018 AV Amsterdam, THE NETHERLANDS.

Verpackungslabor fur Lebensmittel und Getranke
c/o University für Bodenkultur, Gregor Mendel Strasse 33, A-1180 Vienna, AUSTRIA.

World Packaging Organization
1 Vere Street, London W1M 9HQ, UK.

Latin America

Centro Argentino de Servicios y Estudion del Packaging (CESEP)
Hipolito Yrigoyen 850, Buenos Aires, ARGENTINA.

Instituto Mexicano del Envase y Embalaje AG
ANIERM, Paseo de la Reforma No. 122, Mexico 6. D.F., MEXICO.

Middle East

The Israel Institute of Packaging and Industrial Design
2 Carlebach Street, P.O. Box 20038, Tel-Aviv, ISRAEL.

North America

International Development Research Centre (IDRC)
60 Queen Street, P.O. Box 8500, Ottawa, CANADA.

Packaging Association of Canada
45 Charles Street East, Toronto 5, CANADA.

The Packaging Institute
342 Madison Avenue, New York NY 10017, USA.

Volunteers in Technical Assistance (VITA)
1600 Wilson Boulevard, Suite 500, P.O. Box 12438, Arlington, Virginia 22209, USA.

Other useful addresses

A distinction should be made between institutes which will answer queries on food packaging (for example on export requirements for food) and institutes which are able to provide technical assistance regarding packaging and/or marketing of foodstuffs, whether destined for export or not. The following organizations, which are concerned with development issues, may be able to advise on specific problems of packaging:

Agromisa, Intermediate Technology, Natural Resources Institute and *TOOL* (see previous section under Europe).

CIDA
Canadian International Development Association, 200 Promenade du Portage, Hull, Quebec K1A 0GA, CANADA.

GRET
Groupe de Recherche et d'Echanges Technologiques, 213 Rue Lafayette, 75010 Paris, FRANCE.

ITC/GATT
International Trade Centre, 54–56 Rue de Monbrilliant, CH-1202 Geneva, SWITZERLAND.

UNIDO
United Nations Industrial Development Organization, Agro-industries section, P.O. Box 707, A-1011 Vienna, AUSTRIA.

Bibliography

Alles, D. (1982) *Traditional forms of packaging and vending*, Facets of Sri Lanka 1, Seevali Design & Printing Centre, 179 Sir James Peiris Mawatha, Colombo 2, Sri Lanka.

Barail, L.C. (1954) *Packaging Engineering*, Reinhold Publishing Corp., 430 Park Ave, New York 22, USA.

Brody, A.L. (1971) *Flexible Packaging of Foods*, Newnes-Butterworths, London.

Dea-Sung Lee (1984) *The Choice of Packaging Materials for Developing Countries*, Paper: Packaging research and development department, Korea Design and Packaging Center, Seoul, Korea.

FAO World Food Programme (1983) *Food Storage Manual*, FAO, Via delle Terme di Caracalla, 00100 Rome, Italy.

Fellows, Peter (1988) *Food Processing Technology, Principles and Practices*, Ellis Horwood, Chichester.

Fellows, Peter and Axtell, Barrie (1993) *Technical Memorandum on Food Packaging*, ILO, Geneva.

Fellows, Peter and Hampton, Ann (1992) *Small-scale Food Processing: A guide to appropriate equipment*, IT Publications, London.

Griffin, R.C., Sacharo, S. and Brody, A.L. (1972) *Principles of Food Packaging*, AVI Publishing, Westport, Connecticut USA.

Heiss, R. (1970) *Principles of Food Packaging: An international guide*, P. Keppler Verlag KG, Abt. Central-druck, 6056 Heusenstamm, Industriestrasse 2, Germany.

ILO (1986) *Solar Drying; Practical Methods of Food Preservation*, Technical memorandum (WEP), Publication branch, ILO CH-1211 Geneva 22, Switzerland.

Jones, A. (nd) *Packaging problems in India and elsewhere*, Consultant report, UNIDO, Austria.

LIFE (1979) *Packaging Problems in Developing Countries*. League for International Food Education, 1155 Sixteenth St, NW, Room 705, Washington DC, USA.

McDonalds, G.M. (nd) 'Food Packaging; Coffee/Tea and Spices', Consultancy report for PIRA, Randalls Road, Leatherhead, Surrey KT22 7RU, UK.

McDonalds, G.M. (nd) 'Packaging materials', Consultancy report for PIRA (as above).

Milligan, I. (1981) 'Developing new markets', *Packaging Review*, June 1981.

Moody, B.E. (1964) *Packaging in glass*, Hutchinson Publishing Group, London.

Paine, F.A. and Paine, H.V. (1983) *A Handbook of Food Packaging*, Leonard Hill, London.

Paine, F.A. *et al.* (1962) *Fundamentals of packaging*, Blackie & Sons, London.

Ramsland, T. (1989) *Handbook on the Procurement of Packaging*, PRODEC, Töölonkatu 11A, 00100. Helsinki, Finland.

Ranger, H.O. (1985) 'Visiting Experts Help Solve Tough Packaging Problems', in *Packaging*, April 1985, pp.73–77.

Sacharo, S. and Griffin, R.C. (1970) *Food Packaging: A guide for the supplier, processor and distributor*, AVI Publishing, Westport, Connecticut.

Sprenger Instituut (nd), *Guide for the packaging of vegetables and fruit*, Sprenger Instituut, Haagsteeg 6, 6708 PM Wageningen, Netherlands.

Subramanian M.R. (nd), 'Packaging and pollution', in Proceedings of 8th Asia packaging congress.

www.ingramcontent.com/pod-product-compliance
Lightning Source LLC
Jackson TN
JSHW052134131224
75386JS00037B/1272